Entropy Slices

An instruction manual

Holly Crawford

Lokke

New York

Cover photograph by Holly Crawford, 2009

One slice, {S} 096 (under a different number) was original published in *Van Gogh's Ear*, 2nd volume.

www.art-poetry.info

978-0-9852461-2-9
ISBN:978-0-9852461-3-6

For George, my wonderful husband who channels surfs and watches several things at the same time while reading a book on his e-reader. He epitomizes our current world that we create by slicing and dicing information and images that flow by us every second.

And my later father, William C. Shissler Jr., who kindly sent me the manual he wrote on remote handling.

{S}: Entropy Slices

Entropy is usually denoted by the letter {S}. Clausius's entropy was defined for an isolated system in equilibrium which was undergoing reversible processes. "In contrast there is the entropy of Prigogine that describes the behavior of open dissipate structures. Boltzmann's statistical entropy and Shannon's information entropy are mirror images of one another, and this asymmetry causes grief to persons who seek absolute consistency. There is Eddington's 'arrow of time,' which expresses the direction of events and is a foundation stone for the indisputability of irreversible processes. And then there is Kolmogorov's entropy, which describes the deviations between the trajectories of dynamical systems and bears no resemblance what so ever to Clausius's original definition. -- A.B. Cambel, *Applied Chaos Theory*. New York: Academic Press, Inc.,1993.

{S}0000 is used to designate an entropy slice

Instructions and information, things that I have had to deal with and wanted to think about, that have flowed past me. I started collaging them into a narrative of found instructions and bits of history. They are from the following sources: newspapers and newspaper's indices; random instructions from drugs; canned and boxed food and my personal care products; directions to my allergists office (written by her); road signs; rules for entering a poetry contest; computer manuals; receipts; recipes; the complete instructions for the care of living Christmas tree that I bought in 1994; the instructions from pages 45-47 from the Sony Color Rear Video Projector Operating Instructions booklet that I own; pop songs from Billboard; parts of randomly chosen obituaries from several different newspaper indices; quotes from literature, last lines or first lines; part of the dialogue of a movie, *His Girl Friday*, as heard and transcribed by me while listening to that movie once; a Hallmark Cards Inc.- Mother's Day card that I received 5/95; the State Bar of California Approved Health Care Plan Guaranteed Issue Prudent Buyer Plan For Individuals and Their Families booklet pgs 5-6; three discarded and found memos; land excursion descriptions and instructions for tours from a cruise of French Polynesia that I took in 1995; The Bible: Genesis—which had some early instructions; Sections I and II, and the first sentence of section III of Report No. 2307 on Remote Handling of nuclear wastes by my father, William Clyde Shissler Jr.; Shakespeare's *All's Well That Ends Well* (Act II, Scene III) and some of the text from some of the Christmas cards that I received in 1993 and 1994; instruction safety card from a flight I took in 1997--I don't remember which airline; SEC Rule 204-2 ; instructions manuals for the new appliances from a house that we leased September 1, 2001.

Twice I broke the text down into individual parts. First a reading with 12 poets and artists at the Bowery Poetry Club November 2005 and later in 2011 at the Lakeside Theater, University of Essex, UK. One slice was very earlier published in *Van Gogh's Ear* under a different number. It is the same text.

Very early on I submitted a printed manuscript to different poetry contests. More than one hundred pages, one poem per page and many other instructions. And all were experimental poetry contests. I did hear that one year Lawrence F ranked it in the final selection.

Holly Crawford
NYC
August 2012

{S} 0001

Monday
Raiatea
  Oh, Jake,
Raiatea Insight Tour
departure: 7:30 am & 10:00 am
they say miracles are past
more details
$49.00 per person
maximum: 8 persons
duration: 2 1/2 hours
    using advanced features
  decorate me indoors
 I'll be there for you
   we could have had such a damned good time
yes, a South Pacific anthropologist's dream
 you'll always have a special place in my heart
isn't it pretty to think so?

any cancellations must be made 24 hours in advance

{S}0002

hi

{S}0003

hi

{S}0004

please save this for future use

{S}0005

now to make modern and familiar
 the earth was a formless void
the birthplace of the gods
primarily a rest home
 or any like institution
 where the lovely 'Tiare Apetahi' flower grows

{S} 0006

hi

{S}0007

there was darkness over the deep
you can watch, then plant me
to thank you
for all the days when you've been there helping, giving,
caring...

to face things supernatural and causeless
  we have just cut out
the main picture
and services or hospitalization, which begins prior to your
effective date
or after protection has terminated

{S}0008

wait here
 I'll be back in ten minutes
want me to go in with you?

{S} 0009

welcome back

one
 establish procedures
my cat just had kittens
I am a living holiday tree
hence is it that we make trifles of terrors
and for all the days that have been brighter happier, richer...
build a large fleet of boats
 take the culture all over
or continue along the lush jungle
viewing plantations of pineapple, papaya, taro, vanilla beans
and copra
more
see the other side

{S}0010

walk into the past
by ensconcing ourselves into seeming knowledge
under the gaze of all the gods
services provided by local,
 state or federal governmental agencies
the bloodthirsty god of war
who demanded human sacrifices
a little more off the chin
 and the Chinook were largely fished out

{S}0012

 God said,
Happy Holidays
from our family to yours

{S}0013

hi

Happy Mother's Day

{S}0014

hi

hark the herald angels sing
a two hour detailed lecture on history
 entertains you along the way
      for about 5 minutes

{S} 0015

hi

let there be light

{S}0016

Raiatea Snorkeling Adventure
$39.00 per person
departure: 9:45 am
maximum: 36 persons
duration: 1 1/2 hours

hi

I'm retired

{S}0018

hi

{S}0019

Warning!
services or supplies rendered when there is no charge

{S}0020

your guide
 will scuba dive below
to feed a vast array of large colorful fish
get the governor on the telephone
he's fishing

{S} 0024

 Orangutan hybrid bred
the originality of the concept
may I have one and a match
you can
$55.00 per person
what has to be done to remove it?

{S}0025

 God divided light from darkness
thank you
departure: 8:45 am
I cannot see
choose the sound

{S} 0027

since we have seen each other
God called light 'day'
now seen as a pollutant

{S}0029

Please note:
it is recommended
that participants wear long trousers
and the darkness he called 'night'
evening came and morning came
I'm fond of you too

{S}0030

The First Day:

God said,
stay (I miss you)
I'll make love to you

{S}0032

picture an open Polynesian style outrigger canoes
 thousands of newcomers
services or supplies
in connection with investigative or experimental treatment
personal comfort or beautification items

let there be a vault in the waters to divide the waters in two
it is normal for the moisture to collect on the surfaces
 or half the basin

stop calling me

do not set tree on concrete surface
and treatment to alter covered person's physical
characteristics
 to those of the opposite sex;
optometric services, orthopedics,
 routine eye examinations and eye refractions for the fitting of
glasses
 Eyeglasses or contact lenses except as specifically described
in the Benefit Certificate;
 hospitalization primarily for X-ray,
laboratory or other diagnostic studies except where such
services cannot be rendered safely
and adequately on an outpatient basis;
 routine physical examinations
 except as specifically described in the Benefit Certificate;
 hospitalization which is primarily for physical therapy or
treatment of chronic pain;
conditions caused by the release of nuclear energy and
the counting of all plants and animals

not covered.

And the dust and silence on the upper shelf ?
right
and it may leave a stain

God made the window picture
and low voltage lightning
by placing yellow flowers from overhanging "puran" trees
and divided the waters above from the waters under the vault

it's broccoli dear
I say it's spinach,
history tells of larger trees
I truly say it is a novelty to the world
God called the vault 'heaven'

{S} 0036

evening came and morning came:
the second day
departing from the river
select spot next to me

{S}0037

three terrorists and two bystanders,
feel the fluffy softness

{S} 0039

God said,
 let the waters under heaven come together into a single mass,
opportunity to swim, snorkel, relax,
 and let dry land appear
and watch a pareo tying demonstration
you got a better offer

sometimes love
 just ain't enough

{S} 0040

they wouldn't listen Walter

I would have said the very same
for a closer look
bring a towel, hat, mask & snorkel

{S} 0042

God called the dry land
  garden apartments
  and the mass of waters 'seas,'
  and the window picture?

{S} 0043

snorkeling safari
departure: 9:45 am
maximum: 28 persons
$39.00 per person
duration: 2 hours

God said,
display 8 or 16 TV channels
climb aboard this covered snorkeling boat
and cruise across the multicolored lagoon
once you arrive at the coral reef
you will swim amongst the bright tropical fish
and explore the beauty of the delicate coral formations

Why, your dolphin is not lustier 'fore me,
 I speakin respect-
on the other side
let the earth produce plastic vegetation
 it will help keep the floor and carpet dry
except as specifically described in the Benefit Certification
nay, 'tis strange, 'tis very strange
and so it was
simultaneously a private duty nurse
 seed-bearing plants,
and fruit trees bearing fruit appeared
 because I love you
you can also use the ch +/ _ buttons on the remote
be sure to sign out your snorkel gear from the sport's center
that is the brief and tedious of it

release me

{S} 0044

Glass Bottom Boat Adventure
departure: 9:45 am
maximum: 28 persons
$34.00 per person
duration: 1 1/2 hours

news
in as much as this was not part of the original proposal
watch in fascination

{S} 0045

quality is up
burgundy is in
evening came and morning came

{S}0047

hello
the third day
will not appear

{S} 0050

God said,
#3751 is not responsible for
smaller trees and lost shoes
keep this receipt

{S} 0054

let there be lights in the vaults of heaven
this equipment includes manipulators,
viewing equipment,
 vehicles, cranes, turntables, slings, stands, alignment
machinery,
wrenches, power tools, power sources,
continued on the back
you need to know
to divide day from night
The Union Camp Company
 will donate
with the window pictures
services for which the member is not legally obligated to pay
and 50,000 acres in the Dismal Swamp

I lingered round them, under that benign sky;
as to be generally thankful
watched the moths fluttering
away from the heater
 among the heath and hare-bells,
because the company reported
 to the soft wind breathing through the grass;
the land had become unprofitable for further logging
 and wondered how anyone could ever imagine unquiet
slumbers,
 for sleepers in that quiet earth

{S}0060

I'm busy
the display is blocked
general-purpose remote handling equipment can handle it

Bora Bora 4 Wheel Drive Tour
departure: 8:45 am
$56.00 per person
maximum: 24 persons
duration: 3 hours

{S}0062

God made the two great lights
every rose has its thorn
for example
Mighty Mouse cartoon
the greater light to govern the day
is attacked
Is not this Helen?
'Fore God,
 Mighty Mouse
 sniffing cocaine under the guise of sniffing a flower
I think so
go, call before me all the lords of the court

{S}0063

the stars
God set them in the vault of heaven
to shine on the earth
to turn off the lights?
let them cool first
then call

if this is feasible
the manipulator hand grasps the part
lifts the part down
picks the part up
aligns and orients the part of assembly

don't worry be happy
unless opening a window
and peeping through peep holes

and to view the inaccessible spots
you can use the PIP buttons
thanks

{S}0068

when love pleases
fall on the remote

{S} 0069

Look Honey
sacred sites
custom built
discovered by him

{S}0070

nothing gonna stop us now
except as specifically described in the Benefit Certificate:
The Simpsons,
mental or nervous disorders or substance abuse
customs, history, culture
and this warranty

{S} 0071

Bora Bora Island Discovery Tour
departure: 8:45 am
$29.00 per person
maximum: 38 persons
duration: 3 hours
evening came and morning came
the following procedures should be used
I'm particular

The Supreme Court,
in Messe v. Keene,
Tom Higgins, The Nanny, Fresh Prince of Bel-Air
you mind if I meet him
 rules that in designing a bolted flange joint
Congress and the Justice Department marry,
to each other
may label foreign films as political propaganda
when it judges that the films may influence public opinion
 I'm sorry
for other PIP functions
use your "le Truck" vehicle
 and head in a clockwise direction around Bora Bora

{S} 0072

The fourth day

do not pick up tree by the trunk
determine the size of the flange
is this any concern of yours
next time
determine the number, size, and kinds of bolts and nuts

{S} 0073

God said,
we understand
let the earth produce every kind of living creature;
 cattle, reptiles, and every kind of wild beast
The Marshall, baseball, Chicago Tonight, School's Out,
Rockford Files,
The 700 Club
don't worry about it
bring along a few dollars or francs for a cool drink
and so it was

{S}0074

Bora Bora Boat Tour
it looked a little cloudy this morning

I received this book several months ago for possible review
from the Department of Agriculture
Tables 1 through 5,
 approves the first genetically altered virus
to be release into the environment
it determines torque requirements
it's used to fight a form of herpes that affects swine
on white bread
that's what friends are for
and how have things been
maybe you want to submit something

{S} 0078

I can give you back issues
check nut and bolt clearance
determine whether or not dowels,pilot pins,
rabbets, mechanical guides, fixtures,
 or a manipulator are required for the mating of parts
fill the bottom of hole
press off

{S} 0080

Moorea
Thursday
The Senate Committee on Commerce
 begins
4-Wheel Drive Agriculture Adventure

God said,
see, I give you all the seed-bearing plants that are upon the
whole earth
listen carefully
I am here
$53.00 per person
 hearings addressing regulation of all natural products
outpatient speech therapy
and all the trees with seed-bearing fruit
duration: 3 hours
this shall be your food
follow these instructions
for best results use by:
1 pm
a 4 Wheel drive Landrovers depart from the Club Bali Hai

please recycle

{S}0081

Amendment passes
Rung from their marble caves 'Repent! Repent!'
TV/ Video 1,
To My Daughter With Love
Video 2,
Wife, Mother, Murderer
 store in a cool place
or
Video 3
shoe inserts

{S}0084

To all wild beasts
all birds of heaven
 and all living reptiles on the earth
take care
call if problems
my beeper number?
the mountain streams
and so it was
  all the rest is mute

-

{S}0085

the sixth day
backfill around outside of root ball,
dental plates, bridges, crowns, caps, or other dental prostheses
press TV/Video to select the input mode
then on to a private domain

{S}0086

******Please note: the sign-up and cancellation deadline for
this tour is 10:00 pm on Tuesday.

 Press audio

Moorea Island Tour
the display appears for a few seconds
$20.00 per person
you say me say ?
which I won't
man I would
are you sure you want to do this
this is your chance to be a human being
after a short ride to the Club Bali Hai
   buy CBS
please remember that it is normal
thus heaven and earth were completed with all their array
to learn about the life- cycle of the pineapple
and her humble love
begins by examining a fictitious scenario
 in which lifting or grasp points
eyes, bails, trunnions, tapped holes,
and filling any dirt against the trunk,
 and the under side of a flange,
or a manipulator-hand contact point…
 this will gradually kill your tree
 having gone to the very end of an experience
provide rest points

{S}0089

the seventh day
God completed the work he had been doing
to restore the main picture sound
press audio again

{S}0093

scientist have cloned DNA from an extinct animal
remove the part from the assembly
and use normal maintenance procedures
against all odds
(take a look at me now)
and the fever called
'Living'
is conquer'd at last
I'll call back

God blessed the seventh day and made it holy
and so I take my leave
coffee
not for me thanks

{S}0094

next maintenance
pardon me

the tour will now continue backwards

{S}0095

water once a month
only
every breath you take   25 % off
such were the origins of heaven and earth
that relieves my mind

{S} 0096

The second account of the creation

Moorea Helicopter Sight Seeing
$155.00 per person
duration: 20 minutes
first flight 9:30 am

At the time when Yahweh God
made earth and heaven
there was yet no wild bush on the earth
 nor had any wild plant yet sprung up,
for Yahweh God had not sent rain on the earth
nor was there any man to till the soil

However a flood was rising from the earth
 and watering all the surface of the soil
a 20 minute flight aboard a helicopter is available
 for those of you who would like to view

this manual is an attempt to acquaint the designers of the
components,
assemblies, and system with some of the shortcomings of
remote handling
brute force crushes many plants
and to offer a few suggestions

Yahweh God fashioned man of dust from the soil
find fairer fortune,
 if you ever wed

for his father was a snake
yet plants rise again

 The Pyramids will not last a moment
compared with the daisy
 and before Buddha or Jesus spoke
stick around the office
make the connections to your cable converter box as shown
below
these boys are boys of ice,
then he breathed into his nostrils a breath of life,
and thus man became a living being
they'll none of her;
sure, they are bastards to the English;
the French ne'er got 'em
bad business

Yahweh God planted a garden in Eden
which is in the east,
 and there he put the man he had fashioned
the nightingale sang

Yahweh God caused to spring up from the soil every kind of
tree
 enticing to look at and good to eat,
with the tree of life and tree of knowledge
of good and evil
 in the middle of the garden
which, when incorporated in the design,
 will greatly facilitate remote handling

And long after the words of Jesus
you are too young,
  too happy,
and too good, to make yourself a son out of my blood
  and Buddha
simple lost his job shot a cop
and now they're going to hang
  are gone into oblivion
  the nightingale still will sing

Fair one, I think not so
the use of derivatives is examined
nuclear components should never be handled remotely
when manual handling is possible
election coming up
because it is neither preaching nor commanding nor urging
  don't they need another expert
it is just singing

after making the above connections,
turn the cable connection on by the following steps
  which are on pp. 28-29;
then continue
a river flowed from Eden to water the garden,
one inch of pond water on smaller trees
and from there it divided to make four streams
and in the beginning was not a word, but a chirp
-protect from excessive moisture
put your VCR on an inactive channel

{S}0098

news
the second river is named

you will of course have the opportunity to take photographs

{S}0099

preexisting conditions
 Yahweh God took the man
 and settled him in the garden of Eden
to cultivate and take care of it
then Yahweh God gave the man this admonition,
you may eat indeed of all the trees in the garden
 nevertheless, of the tree of knowledge
 of good and evil
you are not to eat,
 for on the day you eat of it
 you shall most surely die
 dilemma
for more information call
1 800 4 SPRING

{S}0101

Yahweh God said,
it is not good that the man should be alone
I will make him a helpmate
 so from the soil,
Yahweh fashioned all the wild beasts and all the birds of
heaven
in quiet neighborhoods
a dog captures a black-footed ferret
and the verse of that sweet old song
it flutters and murmurs still....
  the ferret, was thought to be extinct
the twins were Walter's
these he brought to the man
to see what he would call them
usually you select objects by clicking them once
however to review the remote handling of various parts
 god made the man fall into a deep sleep
 why, how long would it take him....
 assemblies requires consideration
 in the areas of lifting or grasping
 where the points rest
never anything to brag about

{S}0103

let our professional crew
 give you a fun, safe and comfortable ride

the man exclaimed:
I'll be in sealing,
 tool clearances, accessibility and visibility
derives from a thwarted sensation
now   they became one body
but never hope

to order tickets by phone
call me
 no certified check
 no story

now both of them were naked,
yes, my good lord;
  the man and his wife,
 but they felt no shame in front of each other
the window picture moves as illustrated
these areas are discussed below

{S}0104

did God really say you were not to eat from any of the trees
in the garden
   the woman answered the serpent,
by mail, by fax, or in person
we may eat the fruit of the trees in the garden
 but the fruit of the tree in the middle of the garden
God said,
you must not eat it,
 nor touch it under pain of death
these trees will not tolerate it
and seating availability is subject to prior sale
I'll open for a dime

{S}0105

news
another one bites the dust
take off and land from the boat
radiation levels of nuclear plants require that remote
disassembly,
 remote inspection, and remote assembly
 be accomplished in a shop having thick concrete walls
body electric
leave it to beaver
endless love

{S}0106

Reunited
The serpent said to the woman,
 I told you
'No! You will not die!'
not me
no,
 not preceding the covered person's effective date or
until six months after the covered person's effective date
soak it in

{S}0110

God knows in fact that on the day you eat it
your eyes will be opened
 invited to the wedding you will be like gods
swapping input signals with the main and window pictures
The President, can't smile without you
 he was the one they sent to Washington
 He signs a bill
no refunds or exchanges
for complete list of exclusions and benefit limitations
you must read the entire Benefit Certificate

Friday
Mountain Bike Adventure
 I haven't got the time

Federal Communications Commission v. Pacificia Foundation
this machinery consists of overhead cranes, manipulators,
turntables,
disassembly equipment, stands, slings, dollies,
  rules
Filthy Words,
must answer for your raising
I know her well
is obscene
so they sewed fig leaves together
  M*A*S*H wild America
Le frek

-Please tear here...

{S}0115

hi

the Supreme Court
declines to review
Fifty Ways To Leave Your Lover
The case: Castrating the Cat
so he starts hanging around the park
 listening to Muskrat Love

Where are you? he asked,
I heard the sound of you in the garden
I was afraid because I was naked,
follow these instructions to display the main picture
 if it does not appear full when opened,
 it is because contents have settled during shipping and
handling
visibility of the operation is poor
because the operator may be at a distance of 20 to 30 feet,
 but your guide will enthrall you with history,
so I hid
Who told you that you were naked?
 The Governor of New Hampshire
Have you been eating of the tree I forbade you to eat?
 Smokey the Bear died
we'll go to the woods no more,
the laurels all are cut

there will be a brief stop at the Moorea fruit juice distillery
depth perception is poor for the same reason

{S} 0117

 I'm independent
weekdays , 9:00 AM-7:30 PM, EST
the money
the serpent tempted me and I ate
probably won't mean anything to you

then Yahweh God said to the serpent,
Because you have done this
and eat dust every day of your life
nutritional facts?
the beauty of it is
Oh, after I'm gone
seven TV channels appear in numerical sequence

Evacuation Instructions:
listen for directions from authorized personnel

To the woman he said:
I will multiply your pains in childbearing,
you shall give birth to your children in pain
your yearning shall be for your husband,
  yet he will lord it over you
gonna be alright
Moorea Motu Picnic/Snorkeling Excursion
duration: 5 1/2 - 6 hours
departure: 9:30 am
 love will keep us together

To the man he said,
dive "booties" or "aqua socks" are strongly recommended for
foot protection
these examples are analogous to the problems in remote
handling operations
attempting to engage a 1/4-inch bolt 20 feet away
 pull handle
remove rubber
we have been playing for an hour
thanks for everything
 don't thank me
this tour departs from the sports platform,
deck 2, aft

{S}0124

Alt Shift
for example
Departure: 8 am Saturday

.BAT* files: The way we were
mind if I talk to you
I'm just as innocent as anyone else
it's the world after you lose your job
and eat from the tree of which I had forbidden you to eat

hear anything

-now the worst thing

(unintelligible)
 is to go to anything that has to do with the Arts.

 Ya,
 see that- it was (unintelligible)
there was one fellow
he talked about production for use
everything should have a use

 Julie giving that time in the Museum in Jacksonville.

 The Arts you know

may be defined as

- they're Jews,

 they're left wing

- in other words, stay away.

Make a point.

Sure.

what's a gun for...

to shoot
Middle America
- put the word out

- Middle America-type people (unintelligible)

auxiliary, (unintelligible).
Why the hell doesn't Parker get that kind of thing going?

yes
yes
I never had a gun in my hand before

Most of his things are elite groups except,
I mean,
so the cancer thing-
there is nothing crazy about that

maybe nice for Tricia to go up
- ride a bus for 2 hours
do some of the park in Oklahoma

All the virtuous
but my view Bob is to relate it to Middle America and not the
elitist
the joining of any two parts

(unintelligible).

Do you agree?

time's up

Good-bye

good luck

{S} 0125

How do I love thee?
follow these instructions to display
simply press into place
pipes, wires, ducts,
 structural parts,
pressure-vessels components,
let me count the ways
a work may be subject to state regulation where the work,
appeals to the prurient interest in sex;
methods of joining are

soldering, brazing, welding, bolting, riveting, V-type clamps,
 quick-discount couplings, toggle mechanisms,
and others
tie a yellow ribbon 'round the ole oak tree
configuration of joints may be almost anything
in a patently offensive way,
 sexual conduct
Press CH Index 16 to display 16 window pictures
we wouldn't
 wise

I can tell you what
literary artistic, political, or scientific pressure-vessel flanges,
pipes, ducts, and wires
   what's that?
I never said I loved you
 I saw him once
like any human being
and I brought him up to my room because it was warm
 he went away
 each time you press CH Index 16
 however,
the next 16 sequential channels appear
and you'll enjoy picturesque views of waterfalls, pure
mountain streams, bamboo forests, and the temples of
Tahiti's most powerful ancient gods
this discussion will be limited to structures in general
 shame

replaying the main picture as a window picture
flanges are used to join pressure-vessel components, ducts,
pipes,
structures and accessories
the use of flanges permits two members to be joined for six
months
follow these instructions to replay the image
 then you will also have the opportunity to swim in a
waterfall,
 so bring along swimwear and a towel

{S} 0129

Huahine

Sunday
 Yahweh God said,
See the man has become like us,
with his knowledge of good and evil
flanges may be designed to maintain high pressures
 as well as static and dynamic loads
under various temperature conditions
including very high temperature
reason to believe
press replay

{S} 0130

Culture and History Tour
 $35.00 per person
minimum: 8 persons per tour
maximum: 18 persons per tour
duration: 1 3/4 hours
you may reserve these at the reception desk
 please sign up as early as possible to avoid disappointment,
as space is sometimes limited
I will see you on Wednesday, November 8th, at 11:45

I lost my wallet
you'll find a lot of things missing
see esp. Ch's 4-6
so Yahweh God expelled him from the garden of Eden

{S} 0131

Nature Safari
hey wait for me
what about the ethics stuff
I'm on the job
 I put the words down and push them a bit
I want to talk to you
 with the window picture on the left,
and the main picture on the right
get me rewrite
I've got the whole story
what's the story
when using SPLIT,
 vertical lines may appear elongated

back to special attractions
flat-mating flange surfaces containing two guide-pins
and corresponding guide-pin holes have been successfully parted
and mated remotely many times
$55.00 per person
minimum : 2 persons
maximum: 8 persons
 duration: 1 1/2 hours
approximate dimensions were: flange I.D., approximately 6 ft.;
 flange thickness, approximately 1 in.;
 vessel wall, approximately 1/2 to 3/4 in. thick;
 dowel diameters, approximately 1-1/2 in.
 500 dollars to the man that does it
guide pins are used to properly orient mating flanges
you can't blame a guy for trying
and they may assist in the final alignment of mating parts
figures 1 and 2 show recommended design
departure: 9:00 am
then enjoy a 1 1/2 hour guided tour along the beach
 and through coconut plantations
 then select a picture and sound mode
 drop that phone

{S}0138

 production for use,
a rabbet designed into a flanged joint provides shear strength
into the joint
 maybe you're my friend and may be you're not
 and maintains alignment of the mated flanges
 under all loads and temperature conditions
 you can't trust anybody in there
 as well as maintaining alignment of bolt holes
 you don't want to kill anybody
rabbets should have a tapered lead
 to assist in the engagement during assembly
a plain flange without either rabbet or dowels
 and may require mechanical means for aligning the flanges
 during assembly by force
 to their outside diameter
you want to
 I won't let you do that

Flanges may be any shape
like a dog
follow these instructions
 I'm so tired
they do not have to be round
 they may be designed to support static and dynamic loads
 only without the necessity of containing pressure
easy means for alignment and orientation of mating parts are
desirable
see "Alignment and Orientation," section III, G
they know flanges must be properly aligned
 and properly oriented to mate successfully
waking me up in the middle of the night

asking me things
telling me how to adjust the picture quality
 to adjust picture, hue, brightness and sharpness
it's recommended that participants wear long trousers
 don't go
I didn't

  Who pulled the shades down
have a tropical fruit juice
Who are you?
Who is anybody?
call for details

the major portion of the flange aligns the orientation
  and is usually provided by the remote handling equipment
 and may be accomplished by pilot pins
 final closure of alignment may be provided by rabbets
flanges must be straight and free from distortion
or warpage in order to mate properly
and to function successfully camera suggested

 I am not wrong

{S}0142

That you are well restor'd, my lord, I'm glad
transportation to the Sofitel Beach Hotel
let the rest go
round trip
$17.00 per person
this is only temporary
departure: 9:00 am, 9:30 am, 10:00 am , & 10:30 am
return: 12 noon
press the rocker control up and down until the cursor points
to 'video'
   this is not just a story
  you're doing something big
click the rocker control the video screen appears
 you will be transported to the beautiful Sofitel Beach Hotel
where you can enjoy a swim
  we'll let the governor in on it
wear your bathing suit and bring a towel
we got a lot to do

{S} 0143

in the front of the garden of Eden he posted the cherubs,
 and the flame of the flashing swords,

more details

click the rocker control

Holly Crawford is an artist, writer and curator. She is the Director and founder of AC Institute an experimental spaces for research and exhibition in contemporary art (www.artcurrents.org) and publication of books on contemporary art and criticism. She taught art and art issue in the UCLA Art Department and at SVA. She received her Ph.D. from the University of Essex in Art History and Theory, B.A and M.A. in Economics and M.S. in Behavioral Science from UCLA. From 2004-2006, she was a non-clinical Fellow at NYU Medical School Psychoanalytic Center. She was born in California and now lives in New York City.

Selected publications: *Voices Over Art*, Lokke, 2012; *Down the Rabbit Hole*, Lokke 2012; *Buttons, Hooks & Eyes*, Lokke, 2012; *Outsourced Critics*, Holly Crawford, project by & editor, AC Institute, 2010; "Who Gets to Play?' in Popular Culture Values and the Arts Essays on Elitism versus Democratization: edited by Ray B. Browne and Lawrence A. Kreiser, McFarland, 2009; Catalogue essay "Disney and Pop Art",for the catalogue Once Upon a Time Disney, Grand Palais and Fine Art Museum, Montreal, 2008; *Artistic Bedfellows* (editor), UPA/Roman & Littlefield, 2008; "Temporary Bedfellows: Claes Oldenburg, Maurice Tuchman and Disney," essay in *Artistic Bedfellows,* 2008; "Having Their Cake and Eating It Too: The case of Christo's and Jeanne-Claude's Im(permanence) and Exclusivity," essay in *Artistic Bedfellows*, 2008 (conference paper Carnegie Mellon); "Disney and Pop Art", *Once Upon a Time Disney*, Bruno Girveau, (Editor & Curator) Grand Palais and Fine Art Museum, Montreal (two editions-one in French and one in English) Prestel, 2007; *Attached to the Mouse, Disney and Contemporary Art* (2006) UPA/Roman & Littlefield, 2006; "What's New," catalogue essay, DIVA (Digital and Video Art Fair), Paris, 2005.

Contemporary Art Issues Video: *Critical Conversations in a Limo*, NY 2006 (In conjunction with the Armory as VIP project), 2007 in Melbourne (MIAF) & San Francisco (The LAB & Sesnon Gallery UCSC). 8 videos (18+ hours) of discussions about contemporary art

Selected Art Projects:
Her art and poetry (www.art-poetry.info) give new meanings and draws
categories themselves into question through transformative juxtapositions.
Many projects are ongoing, site specific and participatory. Selected
projects: *Offerings* (Ars Electronica, (.net Participant, 1998); *May I have
your autograph?* (unofficial, Basel Miami Art Fair 2007), *Critical
Conversations in a Limo*, NY 2006 (VIP project, Armory), 2007 in
Melbourne (MIAF) & San Francisco (The LAB & Sesnon Gallery UCSC).
Economic Crisis Observatory, (Beacon Arts Building, LA,2012), *Orphans
Offered Up* (2010 NYC, Lakeside Art Gallery University of Essex and
Liverpool 2011); *Open Adoption* (Pool Art Fair 2005*),* Hospitality Suite
(Pool Art Fair 2005), Hospitality Suite, DiVA, Paris, 2005, *Hyphens
(*Gallery 303 NY Photography Fair *&* Brown Bag Contemporary San
Francisco Photograph Fair*), Voice Over NYC to Wels (via Twitters) 2009,*
MKH, Wels, Austria, *Found Punctuation (video)* Tate Modern 2007; *13
Ways of Looking at a Blackbird,* Riverside Art Museum & Florence,
Valencia, London, NYC (The Lab) and Berlin; *The Road* and *Water,
Water, Water,* Downey Art Museum.

Curated projects: *Sound Art Limo,* NY and Melbourne 2007, *Flatland
Limo*, NYC 2008, and *Live in the Limo* was co-curated with Sonya Hofer,
NYC 2009. Curated projects at AC Institute 2008-prsent. Co-curated with
Sonja Hofer 2007-2008; with Sonja Hofer, Joseph DiPonio 2009-2010;
with Joseph DiPonio and Nicole Bebout 2011-2012; Nicole Bebout 2012-
2013.

Member: ACIA

www.ingramcontent.com/pod-product-compliance
Lightning Source LLC
Chambersburg PA
CBHW050947030426
42339CB00007B/330